# MASTERING PEOPLE MANAGEMENT

Based on *Mission: To Manage* by Marianne Page

First published in Great Britain by Practical Inspiration Publishing, 2024

ISBN    978-1-78860-670-7  (print)
           978-1-78860-672-1  (epub)
           978-1-78860-671-4  (Kindle)

Want to bulk-buy copies of this book for your team and colleagues? We can customize the content and co-brand *Mastering People Management* to suit your business's needs.

Please email info@practicalinspiration.com for more details.

**Practical Inspiration Publishing**

# Contents

# Series introduction

Welcome to *6-Minute Smarts*!

This is a series of very short books with one simple purpose: to introduce you to ideas that can make life and work better, and to give you time and space to think about how those ideas might apply to *your* life and work.

Each book introduces you to ten powerful ideas, but ideas on their own are useless – that's why each idea is followed by self-coaching questions to help you work out the 'so what?' for you in just six minutes of exploratory writing. What's exploratory writing? It's the kind of writing you do just for yourself, fast and free, without worrying what anyone else thinks. It's not just about getting ideas out of your head and onto paper where you can see them; it's about finding new connections and insights as you write. This is where the magic happens.

Find out more...

# Introduction

## People management: is it really mission impossible?

Absolutely not! Just like every other role you've ever taken on, it's a series of skills and strategies that can be learned, applied and built upon, day to day, month to month and year to year. As long as you're prepared to work at it and accept that you'll always be learning, you can be a *really* good manager.

## Leader or manager?

There's an age-old question about whether leaders are born or made.

Without doubt, some people are born leaders; they have a charisma and an energy about them that can't be taught or learned and they inspire and lead others.

Equally, you can learn leadership behaviours. You can learn to respect others, to be consistent, fair and direct. Every manager needs to be a leader and every leader needs to be a manager. In your role as a leader, you'll make sure that your team feel comfortable, that they grow as people and contribute to achieving team goals. But people need structure to succeed, and as a manager you need the skills to organize your team's activity and make best use of the resources you have in order to deliver on your goals.

A manager without leadership skills won't optimize their team's potential. On the other hand, a leader without management skills will be chaotic and drive their team crazy.

Great leaders are also managers because they understand the best way to get the work done to achieve their goals.

Great managers are also leaders because they know how to make best use of their own skills and talent and more importantly how to get the best out of every individual in their team to deliver even greater results.

*Introduction*

## Who are you and how did you get here?

I guess this question can be read in two ways:

1. How did you become a people manager? How did you get to the position you're in?
2. What brought you to this book? What are you struggling with or need help with?

Maybe you're a business owner – you started your own business and with success came the need for a small team, that you now feel unqualified to manage. You're doing okay, but you know you can do better.

Or perhaps you were promoted from within the team – the business you work in has grown and your boss needs help in managing the growing team. You were really good at your old job, and you've been in the business a long time too, so you were the natural choice for manager – but you're struggling to find your feet in your new job.

Of course, you could have been hired as a manager. Maybe you've been a manager in another business, or perhaps you did a management degree and this is your first job – either way, you recognize that you still have a lot to learn to put the theory into practice and get the best out of your new team.

However you got here, you'll know more about management than you probably realize. You'll have experienced good and bad leadership, individuals that you'd follow into a burning building, and individuals that you'd cheerfully push into one!

And the truth is, we learn from both.

You're ready to start. Over the next ten chapters (ten days, if you fancy treating this as a mini-course) you're going to discover ten key principles of people management and experiment with using them for yourself.

Let's go!

# Day 1

# Managing stereotypes

There are a few manager stereotypes – you might recognize a couple from your own experience. I like to think of them as types of birds...

## The budgie (everyone's best friend)

This manager wants to be one of the team. They hate confrontation and giving constructive feedback and would rather ignore poor standards than confront an individual, no matter the consequences. They often work late to help out or to correct mistakes the team has made. They still know all the gossip, revelling in their role as agony aunt. Ultimately, they want to be everyone's best friend first and their manager second.

## The woodpecker (micro-manager)

This manager is obsessed with the details – everything has to be perfect and 'just so'. Mistakes get on their nerves because their team should be able to get it right by now. They want reports at every stage of a project and will regularly check up on the team to see what they're doing and that it's being done exactly as they'd do it.

## The peacock (aloof/hands-off manager)

This manager operates from a distance. They give minimal information to the team about what they want and then leave them to get on with it. If things go well they take the credit, if things go badly they blame the team. They're rarely around for advice or support. Always out of the office or in meetings with the boss. They don't get involved in the day-to-day because they don't see it as their job – they have people to deal with all that.

## The seagull (non-stick manager)

This is the manager who swoops in, dumps all over everyone and then flies off again. They're erratic, poorly prepared and arrogant. They damage team morale by treating people like idiots, talking down to them and blaming everyone else for their own failures. When things turn out badly or they run into a problem, they swoop in to assign blame and then become the hero by sorting it out.

## The eagle (inspirational leader)

This is the well-respected manager that the team would walk through fire for. They're inspirational, firm but fair, and hands-on when they're needed. They do what they say they'll do and are always straight with their team, who know exactly where they stand. They give credit whenever possible, and when there's a problem they take responsibility. Always looking to develop their team and better their leadership skills, they have a great relationship with their boss.

They're the leader-manager we all aspire to be every day.

Do you recognize yourself – or your previous managers – in any of these?

## Model the best

One way that we all learn new skills at work is modelling: that simply means looking for behaviours and characteristics that we admire in others, and making them our own. Usually unconsciously, we even adopt the mannerisms, phrases and behaviours of the people we hang round with a lot.

What I'm asking you to do here is become conscious of that 'copying' and choose to model the best behaviours of the managers around you, and stop modelling the behaviours that don't fit you or your values. This is about spotting a behaviour that you admire or respect (e.g. they inspire and they care), and building it into how you behave.

## Learn from the worst

Conversely, there are managers who share several characteristics and behaviours that we want to avoid at all costs. Those, for example, who are bullies, or arrogant, or who abuse their power.

## The four roles of a manager

These are the roles you need to fill to become the manager that your team admires, respects and wants to follow.

## Leader-manager

It's not enough to just tell your employees what to do. Today's generation are not the 'tell me how high you want me to jump' people of days gone by. They want to know why they're jumping, and why this high?

So as leader-manager you need to communicate with, and engage, your team in every way you can, to motivate and inspire your team through your example and your respect for each of them as individuals.

While I do agree that there are some who were born to lead, I also believe that leadership is a skill that can be developed. The context of your surroundings, a particular situation or the people you have with you can also bring out from deep within you the leader that no one knew existed.

- You can learn the behaviours of a leader.
- You can learn to think like a leader.
- You can learn to communicate like a leader.
- You can become a leader.
- Your team needs a leader.

## Manager-coordinator

In this role you look after the nuts and bolts of the job, getting the operation to work as it should, keeping the day-to-day of the operation flowing without a hitch.

Manager-coach

Giving your team the skills they need to do their job well and developing them as people.

Manager-mentor

Take the new employee and train them to follow your systems. Give them all of the skills they need to do the job to the highest standard and develop them to be the best they can be.

As a mentor it's all about helping the individual to become a more rounded person, a great team member, maybe even a leader themselves.

Sharing your life experience (however young you are) and the lessons that you've learned that have helped to shape you with someone who's just getting started, or who's struggling, is a hugely important part of your role as a manager.

## The role of a manager is constantly evolving

In the past you could demand respect, now you have to earn it from your people, from your team. And if you don't... they'll simply move on.

It's important to embrace your own vulnerability, to embrace the fact that you're human and can make mistakes; to be able to say, 'sorry, I got that wrong'.

## You don't lose respect when you're vulnerable, you gain it

These days the most successful leader-managers work *with* their team, using the language of 'we' rather than 'me and them'.

## Management frustrations

The role of a manager has changed, and continues to change and evolve, but there are a few frustrations that many managers can't seem to overcome.

### Frustration #1

How do you get people to do what you say without having to micro-manage them, to cajole them or threaten them with discipline?

### Frustration #2

How can you give somebody feedback that leaves them thinking, 'Okay, I'm going to get that right next time,' rather than, 'I hate my manager!'?

### Frustration #3

When you're promoted into a management role you're very often expected to do the job that you always did in addition to managing people. Like you suddenly turn into a superhero, able to turn an eight-hour working day into a 16-hour working day! (Oh wait... that *is* what you do!)

## How do you manage that?

You definitely don't want to be doing all of your work and all of your team's work.

You don't want to be the manager that nobody listens to and you don't want to let your boss down. You want to continue to be an asset to the business.

You want to continue to progress, develop and improve, and hopefully rise further in the business.

This book will give you the opportunity to learn what it takes to overcome these three frustrations – to develop the skills and understand the strategies that you need to be the leader your team will follow, respected and trusted by everyone you work with, without burning out.

So what? Over to you…

1.  Which of those management stereotypes do
    you recognize from your own experience,
    and what impact might that have on your
    management style?

2. Which of the four management roles feels most natural for you, and which feels most challenging?

3. Which of those three frustrations feels most threatening right now, and what impact is that having on you?

# Day 2

## Mindset and values

### Is management power or is it responsibility?

Decide right now – are you going to be a 'Go' or a 'Let's go' manager? A 'lead from the front' manager or a micro-manager with a big stick?

There are plenty of managers, new and old, who see their position as one of power. But, for me, with the step up to manager comes a big responsibility. As a manager you're responsible for getting the very best out of the individuals you've been asked to lead and manage, to help those individuals to fulfil their potential and to mould them into a team that delivers results for the business.

How you handle that responsibility is going to dictate how well-respected you are, how well your team works with you and how much you achieve together.

## What you believe in matters

Leadership is action, not position. It's what you do that counts, not what you say you'll do.

People talk about values a lot without really understanding what they are and why they're important. Your values are a central part of who you are: who you want to be as a person, as a leader and as a manager; the lines you won't cross in the way you operate; the way you want to be with friends, family and colleagues.

Your values are your internal compass. They guide every decision, every behaviour and every action that you take. When you go against your values, you feel it in your gut.

## What are your values?

When I'm talking about values, I'm talking about the things that make you 'you'. That is, a decent human being. The things that your family, friends and team would say really matter to you. The things that make you angry, the things that delight you, the things that you rail passionately for or against.

Maybe it's your attention to detail. Maybe it's that you always tell it like it is. Maybe it's that you listen in order to understand. Have a go at really *thinking* about the forces that drive you.

## Values lead to culture

The culture of your team will be built around *your* values. Whatever you *show* is important, whatever you measure, whatever you follow up on will be what your team focuses on, will become the things that are important to them too, and ultimately will become the culture of your team.

It's easy to recognize the symptoms of poor culture:

- Lots of sickness and no-shows.
- Sloppy work – lots of mistakes and things missed.
- No communication – and poor communication, most of it on email.
- No respect for each other or the manager.
- Clock-watching.

So what can you do to change a poor culture if you have one, or to create a positive culture if you're just starting to build your team?

As a manager, look at the way you behave, what you follow up on, what you praise, how you communicate with individuals, what you *show* the team is important to you every single day.

## Shadow of the leader

Your team will mimic your behaviours and actions, follow your cues, so model the behaviours that you want to see in your team, because your example will be followed.

## Mindset

Your positive *mindset* has to be backed up by positive *action* and *consistency*.

I believe that people are full of potential. If you show you care about them as a person, they'll try hard for you; if you believe in them and show them that you do, they'll start to believe in themselves and you'll be amazed by what you get back.

Of course, there are exceptions to my positive picture. There are individuals who are just not right for you and your team – but they *will* be right somewhere else, doing something that's perfect for them and their skills.

Everybody has potential. And I want you to feel the joy that comes from helping people to become the best version of themselves,

---

✏️ So what? Over to you…

1. What are your foundational values, the things you argue for and believe in most passionately?

---

2. How might your values translate into the culture of your team?

3. What behaviours do you most want your team to adopt – and how can you model them?

## Day 3

# Positivity and consistency

## Take positive action every day

- If you want to build a high-performing team, what are you going to do today to move one step closer to it?
- If you want to turn round a troublesome employee, what are you going to do today to start building a better relationship with that person?
- If you want to have more influence with your boss, what are you going to do today to show them that you understand what they need from you?

# Be consistent

Taking positive action is a great start, but it doesn't end there. Every team is looking for consistency from their manager, and every manager is looking for it from their team. If you want consistency, then you need to be consistent. Here's how...

## Consistent with your energy

As managers, passionate, positive and enthusiastic people encourage and motivate the whole team, individual by individual. If someone makes a mistake, they'll deal with it quietly and take responsibility with the boss; if someone's done a great job, they'll praise them loudly and make sure they get the credit for their work. Be *that* person. Consistently.

## Consistent in keeping your commitments

Do what you say you're going to do. Respect other people and their time, as well as your own.

## Consistent in developing your team

Give your team the training and the tools they need to take full ownership for their role, then trust them to get on with it, creating a culture of ownership and accountability.

## Consistent in giving feedback

Give honest and constructive feedback. Always. And regularly.

## Consistent in being firm but fair

Lead with your head *and* your heart. Look at things from a position of responsibility rather than power. What am *I* doing or not doing that's causing this? What am *I* saying that's having this effect? When you think about what *you* could do to improve a situation or improve the performance of an individual within your team, you're leading with your head and your heart.

## Consistent in showing your passion for the business culture

Managers gain respect when they're completely bought into the vision and values of the business. They're consistently looking to help the business progress and have a contagious enthusiasm for achieving results.

## Consistent in making decisions

Respect as a manager is hard to win and very easy to lose. Don't be wishy-washy. Understand the values of the business, understand your goals and priorities, and make decisions based on solid information and facts. You may make mistakes, but being willing to make a decision consistently will earn you respect.

### So what? Over to you...

1.  In which area(s) do you find it hardest to be consistent?

2. What's the first step towards putting that right?

3. What's the single most valuable positive action you could take today?

**Day 4**

# Building your team — finding that special person

## Building your team from scratch

Your relationship with any new team member begins before you even meet them. It begins with you working out who you need (that special person) – what role you want to fill, the sort of person you're looking for, what skills and values they must have to fit both the role and the team. This person then needs to be discovered, nurtured and developed, just like any personal relationship you've ever had. In fact, there are so many similarities between the two, let's look at your employee journey in those terms.

## Awareness and attraction

First, you let your ideal partners know that you're available – maybe you tell your friends and family that you're looking for love, or maybe you start going to places where you know your ideal partner may hang out, or, more likely these days, you put your profile up on a dating site, sharing the things about yourself that you hope will attract the right person to you.

How you write this profile is so important. You can't afford to be too modest, to understate the things that make you special, that make you 'you'. But equally you can't tell lies; you can't over-exaggerate or pretend you're something or someone you're not.

Writing a job advert for a team member is just like writing your profile for a dating site. If you want to attract the right person for you, it's vital that you showcase who you *really* are, and why the *right* person will love you and be able to say, 'This one's for me!'

## How to write an attractive job ad

Too many businesses allow the recruitment site to dictate how they present their ad, and too many managers allow their boss to pull together the ad and to manage the hiring process alone, so they have no involvement in hiring this person who needs to be a good fit for *their* team.

For me, a job ad should be made up of three parts:

## Purpose of the business

'Our business is focused on...' This is where you share your business vision, where you talk about what you're looking to achieve, what you want to do for your clients, how you want to help them.

Build the picture of your team – how your team are all focused on what's best for the customer, that you work hard and play hard, that sort of thing. You're looking to get them excited about the prospect of working with you.

## Purpose of the role

'This role is crucial to our success' is a great line to start this section with.

How does this role fit into your business? How does it make things easier or better for the rest of the team or for your customers?

Even if it's a relatively minor role in the business, it must be important or you wouldn't be hiring – so share how important it is to you and the business here.

## Pen portrait

What's this? A pen portrait highlights the values that your new employee will share with you and gives them a feel not only for what they'll be doing and how they'll be doing it, but also, crucially, how they'll be feeling! The job ad should be all about attraction at this stage.

## How to write an attractive job description

Your job description will be attached to your job ad to give your candidate a little more info about the role.

Make it clear and to the point. It doesn't need to be focused on every single detail or every single task that you want this person to do. You could always add a cover-all phrase to your job description that says '... and anything else that we think is necessary to your role'.

The most effective job descriptions are focused on outcomes and results – not what you want the person *to be responsible for*, but what you want them *to achieve*.

We want to get our ideal candidate excited about the prospect of finding their ideal place to work. We want to be as attractive as possible.

## The first interaction – invite to interview

The first interaction with your ideal candidate may well be an exchange of emails. What sort of first impression are you going to make?

Too many businesses show little respect for the people who have taken time to apply for a job with them. Most don't even get the courtesy of a reply to say 'thanks, but no thanks', let alone any feedback about why you didn't feel they were right for your job. Think for a second what it says about your values, to be willing to leave someone hanging, not knowing whether they're being considered or not. What sort of a reputation might you and your business start to get?

It may be a cliché, but you're really not going to get a second chance to make a great first impression.

## The first date – the interview

So, we're at the point now where you think you've found someone who might be right for you – it's time for the first date. In team-building terms, we're talking about the interview.

- How are you going to prepare for it?
- What do you want to get out of it?
- What would the answers to these questions be if this was a first date?

I have two golden rules for hiring:

1. Never hire in a hurry.
2. Never hire to a CV.

When you're preparing for an interview, you need to keep these two golden rules in mind.

But... why? Because when you hire in a hurry there's a good chance you'll make mistakes. When you're desperate, you undervalue the importance of getting things right. Don't settle for the best of a bad bunch – settling is *never* good!

As for CVs, they're also like profiles on a dating site, written to impress, sometimes exaggerated, sometimes bearing no resemblance to reality at all. That's why the interview is so important. That's why preparation is vital.

Think about the questions you need to ask to get beyond the CV and uncover the real person. You want to know what makes them tick, what they think is really important, how they feel they can add value to your team.

Open-ended questions are crucial.

- 'Tell me about a time when you...'
- 'Give me an example of when you last had to deal with an angry customer.'
- 'It says here [on your CV] that you achieved X, tell me how you did that.'
- 'What are you most and least proud of [in your life] to date?'
- 'What's most important to you when you're working in a team?'

## So what? Over to you...

1.  What aspect of recruitment do you feel least confident about, and why?

2. How can you improve your chances of finding the right person for a role?

3. What questions could you ask an interviewee to identify their strengths and potential contribution to the team?

## Day 5

# Dating and living together

### The first invite to meet the family — their first day

I don't know if you remember your first day in a new job — maybe you've had several, maybe you've just had one — but it can often be memorable for all the wrong reasons.

You know, the manager forgot that you were starting that day and you hear, 'Oh, can you just sit there, everyone's in a meeting right now,' or 'Oh, you're here. Right. Great. Um, well, nobody's got time for you at the minute, so if you could just sit at this computer and read through our website...' Yes, really! It happens. Way too often.

Then there are the first days that are so uninspiring, dull and boring that they make your excited new starter feel that they've made the wrong decision, that all the great stuff they heard at the interview and read in the job ad was just talk.

Does your new team member go home inspired, excited and raring to get into day two? Or do they go home feeling unsure whether they should ever go back?

Making a first day memorable is as easy as it is important. Here's how to get it right.

First, you want to make sure that you're fully prepared for your new team member's arrival. You'll make sure the team knows they're coming, what their name is and what they'll be doing, so that they're prepared to welcome their new teammate.

For their induction, I'd always want the business owner (if that's not you) to come and meet my new team member and inspire them with the story of how the business got started, the challenges they've faced, their vision for the future. If the business owner can't be there, make sure you get them to create a simple 'Welcome' video that can be shown in their absence, or sent directly to the new starter's email, to show that they've remembered it's their new employee's first day, and that they care.

Of course, you want to share essential information, such as where the fire exits are, where to get their lunch, what they're going to be working on for their first week, but the rest should all be about inspiration and motivation. You want them going home thinking, 'I can't wait to get started tomorrow.'

So, go forth, and inform, inspire and be prepared!

## Dating – their first 90 days

Your hiring process doesn't end until your new team member has passed their probation, which makes their first 90 days an essential 'getting to know you, warts and all' exercise – just as it is when you start dating someone.

What do you want them to have learned in the first three months? What do you want them to have delivered? What teamwork and personal qualities do you want them to have demonstrated?

During their first week you'll share this with them and then you'll set dates for three important meetings:

- Their 30-day meeting
- Their 60-day meeting
- Their 90-day meeting, which doubles up as their probationary review

These three meetings are as important for you as they are for them. They push you to think about how your new team member is doing – what's going well and what isn't, how you feel they're fitting into the team, what feedback you're getting from the people who are working with them.

The probation period is often underused, with new team members given an easy ride, as you and your team get on with your day-to-day work. Probation is there to fully test their suitability for their new role, to test how they perform under pressure, to test if they're a good fit for your team and your culture. So test them. Give your team member tasks that you'd normally give to someone experienced, ask for their opinion on how to solve a challenge you're facing, put them under (a little) pressure and see how they react.

If they're not rising to the challenge, don't prolong their probation in the hope that they'll become the right person with just a little more time, or because they're 'so lovely'. Instead, let them go, with feedback about what they need to work on, maybe about the type of business they'll excel in, because they *will* be right for another business. Keeping them tied to your team when they're not right is doing you both a disservice.

A probation period must end with a yes or a no decision – don't fudge it!

## Engagement – passing probation

For those who pass their probation, celebrate them joining the team, just as you would (or did) with your engagement. Make a big fuss. Give them something in recognition of the big day – a pin, a sticker, a T-shirt – and get the team together to welcome their new member. Do *something* to show them that becoming part of your team is a big event.

## Who have you got? How to assess your team

Many new managers don't have the luxury of building their team from scratch. Maybe you've joined a business, or maybe you've been plucked from the very team you're now being asked to manage. So how do you assess your former teammates with fresh, objective eyes?

If you could rehire all the members of your team tomorrow, who would make the cut? There are often individuals who have never been right, who should have been weeded out during their probation. Others have never been given the training or, more likely, the feedback they needed, to become a valuable member of the team.

So first, ask yourself the question to identify the person or people who are just not right, because you're the person who's now going to do something about it.

## Potential vs Performance Matrix

Plot your team on a Potential vs Performance Matrix. This matrix gets you to assess the current performance of each individual, together with their potential to improve, develop and grow.

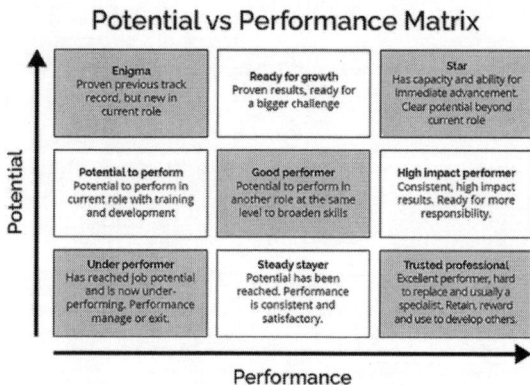

### Potential vs Performance Matrix

| **Enigma** Proven previous track record, but new in current role | **Ready for growth** Proven results, ready for a bigger challenge | **Star** Has capacity and ability for immediate advancement. Clear potential beyond current role |
|---|---|---|
| **Potential to perform** Potential to perform in current role with training and development | **Good performer** Potential to perform in another role at the same level to broaden skills | **High impact performer** Consistent, high impact results. Ready for more responsibility. |
| **Under performer** Has reached job potential and is now under-performing. Performance manage or exit. | **Steady stayer** Potential has been reached. Performance is consistent and satisfactory. | **Trusted professional** Excellent performer, hard to replace and usually a specialist. Retain, reward and use to develop others. |

*(vertical axis label: Potential)*

*(horizontal axis label: Performance)*

## Your people plan

Once you have a clear picture of who is in your team, pull together a people plan that maps out what each individual needs from you in order to become a valuable team member – training, support, feedback, performance management?

Are there skills gaps in your team that you need to fill? Can you fill those gaps by training individuals you already have, or will you need to pull a business case together for hiring someone new? How soon will you need to fill the gap you've identified? And what about the team member(s) who need to go? What's your plan for that? Who do you need to speak to? What steps do you need to take? How will you replace their skills/experience?

## Understanding your team dynamics

Everyone works differently: we communicate in different ways, we want to receive communication in different forms and we get pleasure out of doing different tasks.

The dynamic within a team affects their productivity – whether or not people are 'in flow', meaning the mental state we experience when we're fully immersed in an activity that gives us a feeling of energized focus, full engagement and real enjoyment. If a team is out of sync or out of flow, things happen slowly or, often, not at all.

Different people are in flow doing different things. For example, Manjit might love talking to customers and building warm relationships, while Bill would prefer sitting in front of a complicated spreadsheet looking for the tiny error that he knows is in there somewhere, and Sally is happiest when she's organizing something – people, an event; she doesn't care, as long as she can have a checklist.

Different people also prefer to get their information in different ways. Manjit wants to have a little relationship-building chat before you tell him what you need to tell him. Bill wants the facts… and quickly. 'Just tell me what you need to tell me and then go away.' And Sally? Well, she wants to know the what, the where and the by when of what you're telling her, so that she can add it to her list and give it the right priority.

The fastest way I know of giving people what they need in the way they need it is through profiling (Team Contribution Compass is good). This helps you to understand the profiles and natural energies of the people you manage.

The profile assesses personality, strengths, productivity, values and behaviour, which will give both your team and you as manager the opportunity to focus on strengths and to support each other in areas that you're not naturally drawn to.

Having this information helps you to alter the way you communicate, teach, lead and motivate your team, to get the best possible contribution from each of them. Get this right and you'll have engaged team members who love what they do.

Building a team who share your values and perform to your high standards is your number one priority as a leader-manager.

So what? Over to you…

1.  How can you make a new start's first day a great experience?

2. Plot your team on the Potential-Performance Matrix. What does that reveal?

3. How can you make sure you get the best out of your team by better understanding their individual dynamics?

**Day 6**

# Performance and training

## Training your team is not optional

Without training there can be no consistency, no performance and no ownership. How can there be?

- Your team won't be able to take ownership if you don't teach them exactly what you want them to do and how you want them to do it.
- Your team won't worry about having high standards if you don't give them feedback on their errors and instead correct them yourself.
- Your team won't be engaged in your business if you don't engage with them.

# The learning journey

This has five distinct stages.

## Stage 1: Memorable first day

Now is the time to tell them what the business is all about, the culture, the values, where it came from, why it exists and how much they're going to grow and develop as part of your team.

This first day should be 90% inspiration and 10% information, so give them only the information that they need on day one and leave the rest to day two and beyond.

## Stage 2: Orientation

This is their first week in your business and you want to make it a good one, so what do they need to know straight away, what do they need to learn that's going to set them up for success?

You may want them to know how you operate breaks, where most people go for their lunch, what's expected of them in terms of communication with you and the rest of the team. You may want them to pass a health and safety test or understand your fire safety procedures. Or maybe you want them to spend a day in each area of the business, or with each individual if you have a small team, to get a feel for how the whole business operates day to day.

## Stage 3: First 90 days

For each role, there will be key tasks undertaken to pass their probation.

The key to this crucial period in their learning journey is to test them out with some of the more complex and challenging tasks that they'll be faced with day to day in their role.

These first 90 days give you and your team member the opportunity to work out if you're right for each other, so don't waste them.

## Stage 4: First 12 months

Now is the time to map out your team member's development.

Are there tasks beyond their role that you want them to take responsibility for? Do you want them to learn key tasks of another role to give you cover for holidays?

## Stage 5: Ongoing training

Team training is an ongoing process. With every change, every evolution, every addition to your operation, your team will need training in the *one right way* to perform the new/evolving tasks.

Staying on top of these training needs is a key part of your role as a manager.

## The tools you'll need

### The Team Training Map

The Team Training Map is split into sections that follow the five stages of the learning journey.

Your first task is to identify the different roles in your team. The first box will be labelled 'everyone' – it will capture all the information and training that you want everyone to have.

Once you've identified the roles, you'll begin to map out the training you want each role to receive, in their first week, first 90 days and so on.

**TEAM TRAINING MAP**

| Everyone | 4 days | Rookie (eg Nathan) | 14 days | Pro (eg Joe) | 21 days | Senior (eg Alexander) | 31 days |
|---|---|---|---|---|---|---|---|
| Welcome to [Business] - Video | ☐ | | ☐ | | ☐ | | ☐ |
| Our business culture | ☐ | | ☐ | | ☐ | | ☐ |
| Vision & Values | ☐ | | ☐ | | ☐ | | ☐ |
| Yext deployment | ☐ | | ☐ | | ☐ | | ☐ |
| Tour of the office | ☐ | | ☐ | | ☐ | | ☐ |
| Official induction (Fire safety, ID, forms, Handbook etc) | ☐ | | ☐ | | ☐ | How to revise a document and ask the right question questions | ☐ |
| | | How to revise a document | ☐ | | ☐ | How to review website content | ☐ |
| | | How to use the telephone system | ☐ | | ☐ | How to set KPIs (financial & productivity) | ☐ |
| | | How to answer the phone (scripted) | ☐ | | ☐ | How to monitor KPIs | ☐ |
| | | How to transfer the call to the right person | ☐ | | ☐ | How to give a Performance Review (phone template) | ☐ |
| | | How to record your calls | ☐ | | ☐ | How to recruit (HR) | ☐ |
| | | How to do a risk assessment | ☐ | | ☐ | | ☐ |
| | | How to upload a file to Dropbox | ☐ | | ☐ | | ☐ |
| How To answer the phone & take a message | ☐ | | ☐ | | ☐ | | ☐ |
| How To put an appointment in the diary | ☐ | | ☐ | | ☐ | | ☐ |
| How To send a confirmation email | ☐ | | ☐ | | ☐ | | ☐ |
| How To deal with existing clients | ☐ | | ☐ | | ☐ | | ☐ |
| Key relationship training & how to deal with difficult customers | ☐ | | ☐ | | ☐ | | ☐ |
| | ☐ | | ☐ | | ☐ | | ☐ |
| | ☐ | | ☐ | | ☐ | | ☐ |

What you'll end up with is a complete map of the training required for your team, which initially will double up as a list of How To guides/systems that you need to create!

A system is, after all, just a *simple, logical and repeatable* way of doing something, and there should be only *one* simple, logical repeatable way to do *every* task.

One *right* way.

Is there one right way to do every task in your business? If so, great! If not, then we need to look at how you can get to that point, and where better to start than with the How To guide?

## The How To guide

The simplest, most straightforward way to create a simple, logical, repeatable system is to create a How To guide (How To, for short) in one of four different ways:

1.  The paper-based How To: This is a written, step-by-step guide to completing a task. There should always be a section at the end of the How To that explains 'why we do it this way'.

2.  The infographic: This is a visual representation of how the task will be performed. It combines images of the actions to take with wording for any detail that can't be shown in an image.

3.  The checklist: A checklist isn't often considered to be a How To, but it works well as a summary of How Tos that must be followed in order to complete a bigger task, with tick boxes to ensure that nothing gets missed.

4.  The How To video: This is your secret weapon! Think about it. When you want to learn how to do something new, where is your first port of call? TikTok or YouTube, right?

You want to find a video that shows you how to do whatever it is you want to do – a video is the simplest, clearest and most effective way to get a point across, to give information, to explain the what and the why of a task. Plus, you can pause, rewind and go over the 'lesson' as often as you need to, until you're confident you're doing it right.

## Training system

If you want to be sure that everyone in your team has received the training that you expect, you need to be able to track it, and to do that you'll need to build your training system in a way that allows you to track it.

Trainual is a great app for this, allowing you to store all of your How Tos, policies and team information in one place, and assign specific training to specific roles, exactly as you've laid it out in your Team Training Map.

Effectively, Trainual allows you to create a learning journey for each role, which you can track and measure. This is great for your new starters, and also great for team members who have been with you for some time, as it gives you the opportunity to put them through refresher training to confirm that they're following your 'one right way'.

## How to train your team members

Now that all the tools are in place, you need to know how to train effectively.

Don't simply tell your team to watch what you do, rattle through an explanation at 100mph, get up and leave them to it with an 'okay, got it?'

To train effectively, you need to follow these steps, and train your trainers to follow them too:

### Prepare

Read through your How To guide or watch your How To video to remind yourself of all the key points, making notes if you need to.

### ABC training system

The 1:1 ABC training system that McDonald's always used to train their team members is useful.

A = Attention

You want your team member to listen to what you have to say, concentrating so that they understand, and focused so that they're able to act on what they've learned.

- Ask questions to find out what their existing knowledge is.
- Tell them something interesting about the task they're going to learn.
- Tell them a key fact, a funny anecdote or a tale of disaster related to the task.
- Tell them what the benefit of learning this task is for them.
- Let them know how this task fits into the big picture of your operation.
- Make sure that *you're* not distracted and that you won't be disturbed until you're finished training.

B = Breakdown

Walk your employee through new tasks one chunk at a time, being really clear about what you're doing and why. Think about your pace – too fast and they'll flounder, too slow and their minds will wander.

Get interactive: 'When you get to this point you do X. Why do you think that is?'

C = Check

Once you've taught the whole task in chunks, ask them a few open-ended questions, starting with what, why, how or when.

If they can't answer the questions, go back to the breakdown and retrain each section until both you and they're confident that they've nailed it.

## Practise

Then, when you've finished, let them practise. They also need feedback until they can do the task automatically, following the one right way, and achieving the standard you expect.

# Develop for growth

The best managers start with the foundations – training team members to excel in their role, to perform consistently, giving them the confidence of a productive and valued team member. Then you build their broader skills – the skills that will help them grow as a person. There are several ways to do that.

## Delegation

Many managers dump rather than delegate – getting rid of all the tasks they hate, just because they can. We're back to that power thing!

Delegation will definitely save you time and it will help you to get away from tasks that you don't really need to be doing – that take you out of flow and away from the areas of your job that add most value – but it's also a brilliant way of developing a member of your team and raising their confidence levels by showing that you clearly trust and respect them and their ability to do a good job.

Reasons why managers don't delegate

- **Loss of control:** Often managers won't delegate because they don't want to give up control. They either don't trust the team member to do a good enough job, or they believe their team member may do a better job than they could – and either outcome will make them look bad. These managers are missing the point – the aim is to replace yourself in your current role, to give you freedom and room to grow into your next role.
- **It takes too long:** This is the sort of mindset that holds managers back. It's a really short-term view.
- **My team member will resent it:** This is a cracker! Some people may *love* the task you *hate.*

So don't assume that you're dumping it on them. You can actually say to them, 'I really don't like this task. I can do it, but it takes me a lot longer than it would take you. I know you enjoy this sort of thing and I'd love you to learn how to do this task and take it off my plate.'

## How to delegate

Ask yourself these five questions:

- Can someone in the team perform this task now, or with training?
- Is it an opportunity to develop someone's skills?
- Is it a recurring or routine task?
- Do I have time to delegate effectively? For example, time to train and give feedback.
- Is it a task I *should* delegate? For example, you wouldn't want to delegate an interview or a team member's performance review, but most other tasks will be delegatable, if that's even a word.

So you know you're going to delegate, so...

- **Choose the right person:** This comes back to knowing your team – their strengths and weaknesses.

- **Explain why you're delegating this task to them:** What your reasons are for choosing them for the task, and why you're delegating in the first place.

- **Explain the result that you want:** If you're delegating a routine task, then you'll simply train your team member in the one right way to do the task. But if you're delegating something where only the result is important, tell them the result that you're looking for and empower them to come up with the 'how' themselves.

- **Make sure they have the resources they need:** Do they need any special equipment or software or team support? Set them up for success.

- **Delegate responsibility and authority:** Make sure they know the decisions they can make and those that you want them to run by you. You want them to feel supported in doing the task, but not micro-managed.

- **Give them feedback:** Always check the work you delegated when it's complete, or at set milestones if that's what you agreed. Make sure it was done to the standard you expected, and give your team member feedback – either

to congratulate them on a job well done or to
help them to improve for next time.

- **Say thank you:** Publicly if it's appropriate,
recognizing specific things that they did well,
showcasing to the rest of the team what good
performance looks like.

## Meetings

- You can develop someone by delegating
the whole organization of a meeting series
to them – the venue, the agenda, the
refreshments, etc.
- You can then get members of your team to
present at team meetings. Getting someone to
present to a small group, particularly of their
peers, is a fabulous development exercise.
- Start small, asking each team member to
come to your meeting prepared to discuss
their area, to share what they feel has gone
well, the challenges they've faced since the
last meeting, any wins and so on.

## Mentoring

If you've got somebody who's really struggling in
a particular area – maybe they're an introvert and
they're struggling to be heard in a noisy team or

maybe they're someone with real potential who has a tendency to self-destruct – finding them a mentor outside of the team who's been where they are now, who understands what they're going through, can be a really good way of supporting their development. Or *you* can also be a mentor to individuals in your team. When you see someone struggling, take them to one side, take them out for a coffee, take them for a walk and talk to them about what's going on. 'You just don't seem yourself at the minute. Is everything okay? What you did/said this morning in front of the team – how do you think that made them feel?'

Be a good listener... and that means listening for the things that *aren't* being said – reading between the lines, noticing when people aren't quite themselves. Don't always be diving in there with what *you* think, what *you* believe, what *you* feel is right. Don't always be in a hurry to get to your solution to their problem.

Your example

Every time you walk into your building, every time you pick up the phone to one of your team members, every time you're on a video call, every time you write an email; however you interact with your team, you're casting your shadow over them and they feel your presence.

## So what? Over to you...

1.  Complete the Team Training Map for your team. What does it reveal?

2. What How Tos are you currently using with your team, and how could you make them better?

3. How well do you delegate, and how can you do it more effectively?

# Day 7

## Feedback

Feedback should inspire someone to improve their performance – it should never leave somebody feeling down, feeling like they're no good, like they're never going to get any better.

### Why managers fear giving feedback

- No one has given you a strategy for doing it well.
- You don't give feedback often enough, so you have to build up to every feedback conversation.
- You believe that it's demotivating to give feedback when the team, or an individual, is working really hard, is under pressure or

maybe even has challenges at home.

- You fear the reaction. What if they get angry? What if they get emotional? How will I deal with their response?
- You believe that you can't give feedback to people who used to be your peers, because you'll come across as bossy or on a power trip.

Any of those ring a bell? If so, it's important to remember why you were chosen to be a manager, and the responsibility that comes with being a manager to improve performance, develop your team and help people achieve their potential.

Which, coincidentally, are the three main reasons for giving feedback. So let's tackle the main reasons for your fear and give you a strategy for doing it well.

## Four types of feedback

Here we go... let's look at the four types of feedback.

### No feedback

Giving no feedback at all is more common than you think! Managers may ignore poor standards and fail to comment on things that are being done well. This leads not only to a deterioration of standards, but also to the team disengaging. 'If you don't care, why should we?'

## Negative feedback

This is where you launch into somebody in front of the team, tell them everything that they've done wrong, but don't actually share with them how to put it right.

## Constructive feedback

This is where you tell somebody that although what they've done isn't to standard, you then, crucially, tell them what they need to do to put it right to improve their performance and work to a positive outcome.

## Appreciative feedback

Appreciative feedback is where you tell somebody what a great job they've done, picking up on the specifics of what made it such a good job.

## How to give non-confrontational feedback

Try this three-pronged strategy – I use it at work, at home, in restaurants – whenever I need or want to give feedback.

1. Tell the person why you're speaking to them.
2. Tell them the effect that what you've seen or heard has had or will have – on you, on the team or on the business.
3. Tell them what you want them to change or continue to do.

This feedback strategy is simple – it's focused on specifics of behaviour and not on personality.

## Behaviour vs personality

As a manager you can't change someone's personality (according to one study that's pretty much fixed at the age of five), but you can observe someone's behaviour and then give them feedback that allows them to change it.

We want to give feedback that's focused on how someone has behaved, rather than *who someone is,* in other words 'you did' versus 'you are'.

## When to give feedback

- When you're training someone.
- When your team member has completed a task you delegated to them.
- Any time you spot behaviour that doesn't fit your team's values.
- Any time you see someone deviating from the one right way to do a task.
- Any time you see something that's a great example of the values and standards you expect.

## Create a learning environment

When you're learning something new, you expect to be given feedback. This expectation of training and feedback is known as a learning environment, and when this is created, day-to-day feedback becomes the norm.

## Common mistakes managers make when giving feedback

- Don't pre-empt any feedback with: 'Do you mind if I give you some feedback?' If you've created a learning environment, you'll never need this phrase anyway.

- Don't use the phrase 'constructive criticism'. The word 'criticism' is inherently negative and that's usually how it's then received, regardless of how constructively it's given.
- Don't focus on constructive feedback and give little, if any, appreciative feedback. If you never praise anyone for a job well done, your team may stop trying.
- Don't have a room that you take team members to; if you've created a learning environment and simply want someone to adjust/improve how they perform a task, you don't want to take them too far from their workspace to do that.

Feedback is the most powerful yet sadly the most underused tool that you have in your management toolbox. Make sure that you use it. Daily!

## Giving formal feedback

There are several very good reasons why formal performance reviews are still essential for your business.

- Employees want to know where they stand and want to have their performance formally assessed and reviewed by their manager. It's *their* time with you, and it's precious to them.
- They're great for building rewards around.
- When things go wrong, they're essential in managing someone out of the business who has stopped performing.
- They're a great two-way communication tool.

It's good practice to cover three key areas of performance:

1. **Business assessment:** How well is your team member performing their role?
2. **Time management and personal organization assessment:** Are they meeting deadlines? Are they prioritizing their work effectively to get everything done? Are they responding to colleagues and clients?
3. **Assessment of contribution to the team:** Do they help their teammates? Do they keep others motivated when the pressure is on?

In each area, rate your team member on several specific points. Giving each point a rating, which ranges from Excellent to Unsatisfactory, creates the discussion and gives you the opportunity to give very specific constructive and appreciative feedback.

The most important thing to remember when it comes to a formal performance review is that nothing you say to your team member should be a surprise. Nothing. Ever.

Keep a record of the ongoing feedback they've been given.

When you first start doing your quarterly performance reviews, you'll find that it's you who will do most of the talking. Over time you want that to change, you want to create that learning environment we talked about where your team members are taking control of their own development.

You want to be the person listening – that's when you know that you've really achieved a learning environment, because team members will want to take control of their own development and their own performance improvement.

Give each of your team a notebook called 'My Development Diary', where you ask them to record what they've done well since their last review, what they've learned, any praise they've received, anything they'd like to do for their own development and anything you could do to help.

Performance reviews should have consequences – for good performance and for performance that isn't up to standard. If there are no consequences for the poor performers, the standard of your best performers may well start to drop off. Performance measures are for those who need them, and rewards for those who deserve them.

Rewards don't always have to be monetary; there are plenty of other ways to acknowledge your brightest and best team members and their contribution to the team – giving them greater responsibility, maybe the opportunity to attend a conference, to get additional training, perhaps even promotion to the next level.

## How to receive feedback

Are you open to feedback – from your team, from your boss, from clients?

Do you recognize that you don't have all the answers? That you don't always get things right? That, just like your team, you can learn something new and improve your performance, every single day?

## Agree or disagree?

If you recognize that the feedback given to you is valid, great. Accept the feedback and adjust your behaviour to benefit from it.

If you've been given feedback that you really disagree with, go back to the person who gave it and talk it through – explain your thinking, your alternative view, because the truth is that those of us who give feedback are not always right either. Sometimes we give feedback based on limited data, so it's important to create a culture where somebody can challenge us and our feedback.

So what? Over to you…

1.  What's your natural way of giving feedback? Is it working well?

2. When do you find it hard to give feedback? Why do you think that is?

3. How do you receive and use feedback, and how might you get better at that?

# Day 8

## Communication and engagement

To be seen as a great communicator by your team is crucial for any manager, and it's essential for keeping your team engaged. But what is engagement?

I'd say engagement is when people have real enthusiasm for their work and are emotionally committed to your team and its goals. When team members are engaged, they're productive and they take ownership of their role.

If you don't master your communication skills, you'll have little chance of engaging your team. And if you don't engage your team, then every day could be a struggle.

## Common mistakes

Here are the seven most common mistakes managers make.

### Mistake 1: Not communicating enough

One of the biggest complaints I hear from teams is that they don't know what's going on in the business: many managers believe that information should be given on a 'need to know' basis. But if you keep your team in the dark, you miss out on the trust that comes from transparency and the engagement that comes from a belief that we're all in this together.

If you want to know what to communicate and what not to communicate, ask yourself these questions:

- Is it confidential (competitive information, maybe)?
- Is it personal (for example, to an employee)? *Never* gossip with your team!
- Is it harmful (to an individual, for example)?

If the answer to all of those questions is no, then share the information with your team.

## Mistake 2: Underestimating your team's knowledge and ability

Everyone who comes to work with you is full of potential, has their own motivation and is usually smart, and it's up to you to engage them in a way that draws the very best out of them.

## Mistake 3: Lying

Lying is a dangerous game for a manager to play, regardless of the motivation for doing it. Lies have a way of being uncovered, and there's no quicker way to lose trust and respect than to be caught in a lie. Be straight with your team.

## Mistake 4: Being unapproachable

Many managers wrongly believe that to be a good manager they have to be aloof from their team but as a communication strategy this is disastrous. All the communication is one-way – from you to the team – and certainly not delivered in a productive manner. Problems and challenges are left unresolved because your team members don't see any point in raising them.

## Mistake 5: Being too approachable

It's also possible to make the opposite mistake and encourage your team to become reliant on you. You want your team to think for themselves and you also want to protect your own time while giving your team the time and the input they need.

## Mistake 6: Overusing email

- **Don't** send an excess of emails that require an almost immediate response, regardless of the day or time they're sent.
- **Don't** hide behind email rather than being straight and having that honest conversation face to face.

Emails can cause all sorts of communication problems. Email bullying (intentional or not) is a very real threat in every workplace. Instead, create a culture of open and honest face-to-face communication.

## Mistake 7: Believing that 'I sent an email' is enough

Don't assume they've read your email. Take into account possible technology glitches, or an overfull inbox, or simply the fact that different individuals in your team have different communication preferences.

Email should never be the only method of communication used.

# How to communicate

Okay, let's talk about how to communicate *well*.

## How to become a great communicator

Communicate in line with your values and stay true to what's important to you.

We all do things at times that go against our values and leave us feeling cross with ourselves – you feel it in your gut. When you communicate in line with your values, you feel really good about yourself.

## Learn to be more self-aware

Being self-aware helps you to be true to yourself, to be more open and authentic in your communication, to understand your successes and failures, and what you need from your team to complement or make up for the skills you have or don't have.

Every week set aside up to 90 minutes to reflect on your communication over the previous seven days:

- What was I aiming to achieve?
- What went well, and why?
- What didn't, and why?
- Did I do anything or say anything that wasn't in line with my values?
- What lessons have I learned about myself this week?
- What am I going to do better next week?

Being known for your willingness to listen brings you closer to your team – it shows you care.

- Be attentive and completely engage in the conversation.
- Listen to the body language as well as the words. Look for clues as to how they're feeling. And watch your own body language too – keep it open and maintain eye contact.
- Repeat back the gist of what you hear, to confirm that you've been listening and that you've understood the point your team member is making.

- Ask questions to clarify your understanding.
- Be measured in your response, and if you want more time to think things through, agree a time to get back to them.
- Admit when you don't know something or when you're wrong.

Owning a mistake or admitting that you don't have all the answers will actually grow your respect with your team. You'll be amazed at the number of brownie points that earns you with the team.

## Ask for feedback

'What can I do better to help you improve your performance?' is a great question to ask your team members, particularly during performance reviews and one-to-ones. 'What blockers can I remove that will help you to operate more efficiently/give our clients a better service?'

These questions all show your team that you care, that you know you're not perfect and that you value their opinion. Of course, you then have to reflect on and respond to their feedback, acting on it whenever possible.

## Have some fun

Some of the most productive teams I've ever worked with put having fun right up near the top of the agenda, and there are loads of studies out there that will tell you that a happy team performs way better than an unhappy one. So, get to know your people, be kind and be consistent.


## How to communicate with a virtual team

A virtual team will have many of the same communication needs as an in-house team. Keep them included and involved – you don't have the luxury of giving that 'in-passing' feedback that you give an in-house team member. Agree set protocols for how and when you'll communicate, and then be disciplined in sticking to them.

Jumping on a video call or sharing files is easy these days, and Slack and WhatsApp are helpful in keeping information flowing between all members of the team. And, of course, the telephone still works too!

Aim to treat a virtual team member in exactly the same way as a face-to-face team member – same performance measures, same goals and deadlines, same communication.

## How to communicate change

In every business, things change, stuff happens, and it's your role as a manager to keep your team up to speed with what's going on, to manage the change so that they're not unsettled by it, and to keep everyone positive as far as you possibly can.

Communication is everything when it comes to managing change. Here are six top tips for getting it right:

1. Be very specific and very clear about what's changing and why.
2. Think about who might be affected emotionally by the change, and speak to those team members individually.
3. Tell your team the good news – what's in it for them, what the benefits are of changing. And if there is no good news, tell them that too, and thank them for their patience while you do what has to be done.
4. Paint a clear picture of what will happen when, and manage their expectations in terms of any timeframes.
5. Make it clear what, if anything, you need your team to do and get them involved whenever you can.

6. Give anyone who has concerns the opportunity to come and talk to you one-to-one.

## How to communicate with your boss or your team through a presentation

Presenting well to a group is a great skill to develop. Here are some useful tips.

### Preparation

As with your meetings, planning and preparation are everything when it comes to presentations. Ask yourself:

- What are the (maximum) three key messages I want to get across? If my audience were to walk away with only one key message, what do I want it to be?
- Who am I presenting to? Are they interested in what I want to talk about?
- Put yourself in the shoes of your audience and make sure that you have the answers to the questions that you know they'll ask.
- Keep your presentation simple and brief.
- Practise! Test your presentation out on a colleague, or at home with family or a friend.

Delivery

Structure your presentation into these three simple parts:

- Tell them what you're going to tell them.
- Tell them.
- Tell them what you've told them.

Questions

If you're asked something that you haven't thought of and you don't know the answer to, admit it: say that you'll find out and get back to them, and then make sure that you do.

To be a good manager, a manager who connects with and engages their team, you must first master your communication skills, and then build a rhythm of communication that your team can rely on.

So what? Over to you...

1. What communication mistake are you most prone to, and how can you improve?

2. How could you bring more fun into your team to build engagement?

3.  If you have virtual team members, how are
    you ensuring that (two-way) communication
    works well?

## Day 9

# Planning and routines
# (you, me, them)

I love the 90-day planning cycle!

Working with 90-day goals keeps you focused, keeps you moving forward and gives you the chance to tackle challenges and grab opportunities as they come along, adjusting your plans for the next 90 days to accommodate them. They'll ensure that you achieve your 12-month goals.

## How to set your 90-day goals

- Meet with your boss to agree priorities for your team for the next 90 days. What are the three biggest priorities? Confirm these in writing.

- Before meeting with your team, spend some time thinking about your goals and the role that you want individuals in your team to play in delivering them. Be open to your team's input and ideas.
- Meet with your team to share your goals and to discuss your plan for delivering them. What are the biggest priorities? What are the individual actions? Who 'owns' the action?
- Agree dates for your next 90-day meeting, the goal review and update meetings at 30 and 60 days.

## Your communication system

Agree the plan, communicate the plan, follow up at regular set intervals to ensure that the plan is being implemented day to day, week to week, month to month in a rhythm of continuous forward momentum.

## How to run effective meetings

A really good way to get focused for your meeting is to ask yourself six questions starting with why, what, when, where, who and how.

1. What's the purpose of the meeting?
2. Who needs to attend?
3. When is the best time to meet?
4. Where will we meet?
5. How will we run the meeting and how long should it take? (The average attention span is about 40 minutes so keep meetings as short as possible!)

By the end of the meeting your aim should be to have achieved what you set out to achieve, with everyone feeling that they've been heard, and fully committed to the agreements and actions, even if they didn't fully agree.

## Meetings that will give your team rhythm

**The daily huddle:** Short and sharp, and a great way to keep everyone engaged and involved.

**The weekly team meeting:** A more formal review of what's been achieved in the week, and a preview of the coming week's activity and goals.

**The 90-day planning meeting:** A key meeting in the team's calendar four times a year, with the last meeting doubling up as the annual planning meeting, and team celebration!

## Your routines and rituals

### Routines

Routines help you get things done that need to be done at a set time – every day, every week on the same day, every month.

- **Team meetings:** As we've discussed, I'd recommend you start there.
- **Operational routines:** Reports, short-term and long-term planning.
- **The start-of-the-day routine:** This may include ticking off items on a checklist such as switching off the alarm, turning on the lights, turning on the photocopier and checking the paper stock, etc.
- **The end-of-the-day routine:** Do you have a closing checklist? Maybe you want everyone

to spend the last 15 minutes of each day reviewing what they've achieved and planning for the next day.

## Rituals

Rituals help to develop your culture and engage your team. They could be:

- **Milestone celebrations:** This might be to link your 90-day planning and goal review meetings with pizza for the team – so your ritual would become 'planning and pizza'. Or a work anniversary to mark years of service. And then of course there are birthdays.
- **Superhero of the week:** Recognizing someone who's done something special, either for the team or a customer.
- **First-day ritual:** Taking a new starter out for lunch on their first day to show the new team member how much you value the people in your team.
- **Monthly lunch-and-learn sessions:** Interesting topics that most of the team will benefit from.

### So what? Over to you...

1.  How might a 90-day planning cycle work for you and your team?

2. What are your personal and team routines right now? How could you build on these?

3. What are your personal and team rituals right now? How could you build on these?

# Day 10

## Personal management

As a manager you need to protect your own time and energy. So how do you keep all the plates spinning – keep all the balls in the air – and still have a life? Remember what they tell you in the safety briefing every time you fly – always put your own oxygen mask on first!

You need to develop a personal management system that protects your time, protects your energy and allows you to get your work done – to give what you need to give to your boss and your team.

### How to get past overwhelm

We all have days where we feel overwhelmed – as one-offs, these days are manageable. But when these days start to merge, and when (as one manager said to me) 'overwhelm becomes the norm, when you forget where the hell you're going, let alone how you're going to get there', that's when overwhelm has become a real issue.

Try this 'My Big List' exercise:

1. Decide on the timeframe that's overwhelming you. Is it what you have on today, tomorrow, the coming week, the coming month?

2. Next, get yourself a big sheet of paper and a pen and write down everything that you believe you have to get done in that time period.

3. Write down everything – and I mean *everything* – you believe you have to get done in the coming week; personal, business – everything!

4. Once you've done that and you're sure you have it all on that sheet of paper, grab a big black marker pen.

5. Go through your list and cross off everything that doesn't move you towards what you're trying to achieve, everything that doesn't move you towards your 90-day goals, everything that isn't important to your personal relationships.

6. There will be things on your list that do have to be done, but don't have to be done by you – move these onto a second list, called 'to delegate'.

7. What you're left with after this exercise are three lists:

   - Your **Do** list – the things you're going to do because they move you towards the achievement of your 90-day goals, including your own personal goals.

   - Your **Ditch** list – full of other people's stuff, and things that you've just got into the bad habit of adding to your list every day.

   - Your **Delegate** list – things that you're going to get other people to do.

## How to prioritize

Prioritize your list using the Urgency vs Importance Matrix, which helps you to get really clear about what you must do and in what order. As you can see, the matrix has four boxes to hold your tasks.

| IMPORTANT but not urgent | URGENT and IMPORTANT |
|---|---|
| Spend time over these tasks and do them carefully | Do these tasks now and do them thoroughly |
| Do not waste any time on these tasks | Do these quickly to get them done |
| Not important and not urgent | URGENT but not important |

**Top left box:** All these tasks are very important (e.g. putting the agenda together for your next monthly team meeting) – you need to spend time on them – but you don't have to get them done *right* now!

**Top right box:** Tasks that need to be done now, and they need to be done thoroughly (e.g. a client has complained about one of your team and has asked you to call him – urgent and important).

**Bottom right box:** Tasks that you need to get done and done quickly, often because they're in one of your team's or your boss's urgent and important box.

**Bottom left box:** The final box is for tasks that are neither important nor urgent (e.g. 'read emails I've subscribed to').

## Remember your rhythm

I talk a lot about starting your day *on purpose* – knowing what you want to achieve (your three things or your one thing), understanding how what you achieve today will move you one step closer to achieving your 90-day goals and your goals for the year.

Plan your week at the end of the previous week to decide what you absolutely have to get done and what you're going to get done by the end of the week. Then, every evening, invest another 10–15 minutes planning the next day so you hit the ground running, clear about what your *one thing* is going to be.

## Batching for improved focus and productivity

Multitasking is a lie! We can *do* two things at once, but we can't *focus* on two things at once. If you were walking across a tightrope, 30 feet in the air, you'd stop talking, wouldn't you?

So how do you stay focused? One of my top tips for productivity is batching, or pulling similar tasks together and doing them all in one time period – like the way most people do their household shopping.

Why? Rather than flitting from one task to another, having to refocus every time you change task – from something creative, such as writing a blog, maybe, to something that requires more analytic thought, such as pulling together a report – batching allows you to get in the right mindset and increases both your productivity and the quality of your work.

As a manager, batching is all about gathering similar tasks together and doing them all within a set timeframe, without any distraction, to maximize your focus and your productivity; for example, batching your team member training sessions together, preparing your team one-to-ones in one batch of time, batching calls to clients, batching your email answering.

Match the batching! Think about what time of the day you work best and use that time to work on similar tasks. For example, I work best in the morning so if I'm going to work on my financials then I'll plan that into my day early so I can leave a good chunk of the day to do something more creative and fun that I naturally have more energy and enthusiasm for.

## Teach your team how to work with you

Many managers believe that they have to be available for their team every minute of every day. They've heard how good managers have an open-door policy, and they don't want to shut their door and turn the team against them. However, consider these two points:

1. Is there a training need here? Do the people who keep coming to me with questions not know the answers because they haven't been trained well, or at all? Or...
2. Is there a confidence issue? Does this team member know what they need to do and how, but just want the reassurance of always double-checking with you?

If your answer is number 1, it's a training issue, and you clearly need to set aside time to do some training or delegate the training to one of your trusted senior team members.

If your answer is number 2, then there are two parts to your strategy for dealing with these interruptions:

- **Part A** is to get your team together and tell them that you're happy for them to come to you with questions and problems, but that they should try to consider possible solutions first.

- **Part B** is to set aside a couple of hours in the day for 'team time', where individuals can come to you with any questions they have, or challenges they're facing with their work, or maybe outside of work, that are affecting them personally. Issues or blockers raised in the daily huddle can also be dealt with here.

## How to get control of your biggest time vampire

The biggest time vampire for managers is their inbox, and many people lose whole days to it!

### Reframe

Reframe the way you think about your inbox. There's very little that's life and death or business-threatening in your inbox – nothing that can't wait an hour or two. If something was that urgent, you'd get a call.

## Switch off your notifications

This may be very difficult if you like to feel connected all the time, but worth it if you're looking to protect your time and be more productive.

## Check and deal with emails twice a day

Remember your batching, and set two time slots a day where you check and deal with your emails. Put an automated message on your email that tells anyone who contacts you, and then stick to it. Be disciplined.

## Follow the four-folder strategy

When you're working in your inbox, ask yourself these questions:

1. What does this email mean to me and why do I care? Is it important to me?
2. What action do I need to take? Do I need to take any action?
3. What's the best way to deal with this email and its content? Do I have to do anything?

Then, based on the answers to these questions, put each email in one of these four folders:

## Folder 1: Action required

For emails that need you to complete a task or follow-up. Add these tasks to your Urgency vs Importance Matrix in the appropriate box and visit this folder at a set time every week to archive emails containing tasks that have been completed.

## Folder 2: Awaiting response

For emails you expect important responses to, maybe from a client, a team member or your boss. Again, visit this folder every week. Did you get the response? Does that response mean there's now an action required? Does the email string now need to move to the action required folder?

## Folder 3: Delegated

For emails you've delegated to others. Use your delegation worksheet to keep a track of what has been delegated and to whom, and when the task needs to be completed.

## Folder 4: Archived

For emails you want out of your inbox without deleting them completely. If you want to get your inbox to zero:

- Delete – ask: 'Is this relevant to me?' 'Am I just cc'd?' 'Is it something in the four folders that I can now get rid of?'
- Do – ask: 'Can I deal with this in two minutes?' If so, do it, do it now and don't put it off.
- Defer – ask: 'Will it take longer than two minutes?' 'If so, which of the four folders does it belong in?'

## How to manage your relationship with your boss

Just as you need to know your team well in order to manage them, you need to know your boss well in order to build an effective and enjoyable working relationship.

- Are they visual, or do they prefer spreadsheets?
- Do they want the whole story or just the facts?
- Are they big picture, or do they want every detail?

## Tips for a great working relationship with your boss

Be the manager that your boss can rely on to get the basics right. Be the consistent person who shows up on time, works effectively, completes their work to a high standard and, of course, meets deadlines.

## Understand their goals

What's your boss looking to achieve and what are their priorities? If you've worked with them to set your 90-day goals, this should already be clear. Make sure that you're on the same page and that you, your boss and your team are all pulling in the same direction.

## Communicate regularly and effectively

Even if you see each other every day, make sure that you agree a time each week where you sit down and have a formal meeting, just as you would with your team.

## Don't be afraid to challenge

Try this: 'That sounds like a great idea, and of course I'm happy to work on it, but I'm currently working on this, this and this as a priority – which of these would you like me to delay/drop/put on hold to make room for this new task?'

In this way you're remaining positive but also asking your boss to determine the real priority. Often your boss will decide that their new idea can wait a while. When this happens, make a note of it, so that you can bring it up in one of your catch-up meetings further down the line, to show that you haven't forgotten it.

## Be the manager you would want to work with

Be someone who brings you solutions to problems, not just problems. Someone who anticipates what will be needed and acts quickly. Someone who keeps challenges with the team away from you and keeps the team engaged, positive and productive. Someone who delivers results. Someone who is always honest and tells it like it is, even when it's not what you want to hear. Someone who has your back and is loyal to you and the business.

## Build the relationship

Remember that your boss is a human being who will make mistakes, have off-days and do things that make you mad as hell. When these things happen, take a breath. Just as you would with your team, when you notice they're stressed or frustrated, talk to them, show an interest, show that you care about them as a person. Be friendly, but not best friends – maintaining that little bit of distance shows respect for their position and gives them room to make the difficult decisions when they need to.

## Know your numbers

At the very least, you need to know the key performance indicators (the most important measures of performance) for your business, but you'll add even greater value when you also understand and manage the following:

- The critical performance measures for your team.
- Your team's targets and your performance against them.
- Your team's contribution to business revenue as a whole and per person.
- Your team spend – on travel, on photocopying, on office supplies. Are expenses going up or are they under control?
- Ways to simplify and streamline your team's operation.

Focusing on these will help make conversations with your boss more effective.

Your time and energy are very precious. It's vital that you protect and manage both. Don't forget to put your own oxygen mask on first! Develop an effective personal management system and then master it.

## So what? Over to you...

1. What's at the top of your Do/Delegate/ Ditch lists?

2. What's your biggest productivity suck, and how can you manage it differently?

3.  What one change will most benefit your relationship with YOUR manager?

# Conclusion

Successful leader-managers understand the need to keep learning and to find learning opportunities in a wide variety of places – through books, through learning new skills, through self-study, through work-sponsored programmes. They learn from their employees, their peers, their boss, and may even find themselves a mentor.

Successful leader-managers all share a passion for continuous improvement and continuous learning – for new skills and new ideas.

Successful leader-managers understand that learning isn't just about business skills. A good manager will network with other managers, face to face and online. They'll listen to what's going on in the business world and look for new ideas in other industries, new technologies and new ways of working that they could try out or adopt with their team, for the benefit of the business. They'll listen to their customers, monitor social media channels and learn through their day-to-day communication.

## Conclusion

When you take your personal development seriously, when you champion the idea of self-improvement, growth and learning, then your team will see you doing this and be more likely to take their own growth and personal development seriously. They'll become more motivated, more educated, and both you and they will find more ways to improve your business and contribute to its growth.

Here's to being the manager you want to become – one day at a time!

# Enjoyed this?
# Then you'll love…

*Mission: To Manage: Because managing people doesn't need to be mission impossible by Marianne Page* Master the seven essential management skills to become the leader your team want to follow.

Why is it that so many managers see the challenge of managing people as mission impossible? Is it because people are impossible? Is it because they're all inherently lazy, or stupid, or out to undermine you?

No. People are full of potential and passion – they want to be engaged in what they're doing and valued for doing it well. So how can you tap into this passion and potential to become the leader your team want to follow?

The answer lies in the seven essentials that every manager must master to engage their people and build them into a high-performing team.

*Mission: To Manage* challenges the reader to examine their mindset around managing people and to master the skills and strategies essential to success in their new role. While sharing the theory, *Mission: To Manage* is all about implementation and action, focused on sharing tips, strategies, worksheets and quick wins that can be put into practice immediately, giving the manager both the strategies and the confidence to become the leader their team want to follow.

**Marianne Page** is an award-winning leader and developer of high-performing teams, inspiring successful small business owners to build the simple systems and high-performing team that will free them from the day to day of their operation, giving them back the time to enjoy a fulfilling life, confident that their business is running as it should.

Marianne developed a number of high-performing teams of her own during her 27-year career as a senior manager with McDonald's, and developed over 14,000 managers and franchisees over an eight-year period as the company's Training Manager.

Her mission is to give every business owner and manager the tools and the mindset they need to build a scaleable business with a highly engaged, high-performing team to run it.

# Other 6-Minute Smart titles

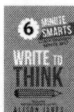

*Write to Think* (based on *Exploratory Writing* by Alison Jones)

*No-Nonsense PR* (based on *Hype Yourself* by Lucy Werner)

*Do Change Better* (based on *How to be a Change Superhero* by Lucinda Carney)

*How to be Happy at Work* (based on *My Job Isn't Working!* by Michael Brown)

*Present Like a Pro* (based on *Executive Presentations* by Jacqui Harper)

Look out for more titles coming soon! Visit www.practicalinspiration.com for all our latest titles.